A DREAMER'S JOURNEY

Dr. Phyllis Baker

Educa Vision, Inc.

For information, please contact:
Educa Vision Inc.,

7550 NW 47th Avenue
Coconut Creek, FL 33073
Tel:(954) 968-7433
E-mail: educa@aol.com
Web: www.educavision.com
ISBN:1-58432-471-6
Cat# B504

Table of Contents

Cover: "Dreams from Beyond," Philippe Dodard

ACKNOWLEDGEMENTS

I want to honor my family Bobby, Brian and Robert Baker, whose love and support has made it all possible. I would like to thank my Editor, Ruby Moaney for flying to Miami and facilitating our very productive, marathon editing session. Her editing skills, overall, have proven invaluable to me. I must thank Dr. Carole Boyce-Davies and Babacar M' Bow for also helping me with this manuscript, and for their friendship, and additionally for providing the intellectual community whereby this work is possible. I would like to extend my appreciation to Theresa Jenoure for reading this manuscript and offering valuable insights. Many thanks to Gregory Williams for his inspiration and friendship. I am very indebted to and would also like to acknowledge the brilliant artist Philippe Dodard from Haiti for agreeing to allow me to use his artwork in this book.

"WHO IS THAT SPIRIT THAT BEHOLDS THE
WONDER OF DREAMS?
... IN DREAMS THE MIND BEHOLDS ITS OWN
IMMENSITY"

Pippalada, Prassna Upanishad

A Dreamer's Journey to Discovery

Introduction

Your dreams are calling you, beckoning for you to listen, to pay attention, and to grasp the scenes of the sixth sense. The movie plays night after night and day after day, but most of it you do not comprehend. I say most of it because I believe some of the data is registered and recorded in the subconscious even if we are not fully aware of its full content. Evidence of this is the different moods we experience and encounter when we awaken. We do not feel the same every day. Some mornings we awake full of life, energy and optimism; sometimes we are at the edge of despair. Other days are average, neutral, and uneventful. We are complacent when suddenly we are prompted to call a friend, see a movie, or do something meaningful. We feel impelled to seek, pray, or engage in spiritual disciplines. What accounts for these different feelings, moods and inspiration when we awake? Are our dreams communicating something deep within us even if we do not fully understand exactly what it is? Be the dream as it may, many times there is no denying that it signals some work must be done. Be stronger, be wiser, be fruitful...help, move, progress, achieve, heal...our dreams beacon, inspire and encourage us to move. In this vein dreams can not be ignored.

The purpose of this book is to reveal the messages in our dreams. To make the dreams clearer, the imagery sharper and ultimately our psychological and spiritual work easier and more effective.

Human beings, by our very nature, have gaps in understanding. At times we are lost and confused. We experience various forms of emotional and spiritual disorientation, which we may or may not recognize and acknowledge. Many times this is attributed to our subconscious and conscious levels of mind. One is out of synch with the other. In a sense the right hand does not know what the left hand is doing. There is a disconnection within our psychic structure that causes us depression, anxiety, illness, emotional and psychological blindness and pain. As a result, we do not live up to our potential, enjoy life and be all that we were called to be. Dream work can be a mechanism for achieving transformation and wholeness. We all have work to do, and our dreams can help us do our work, and live our lives with joy in a myriad of miraculous ways. The focus of this book is to understand how and to help us assimilate, synthesize and interface our lives so we can be better and more fulfilled human beings.

Come ride with me as we take this dream journey together. You have already purchased your ticket by obtaining this book. Now pack your bags. In your luggage, make sure you include:

1.   <u>An open mind.</u> You must be willing to say "yes" to your higher self   (also referred to as "your friend"). We have so often said *yes* to materialism, yes to rationalism, yes to science, anger, greed, lust, pride, people, and in many cases we are still lost. Why not try to say *yes* to the collective unconscious, the great one? Why not say *yes* to this invisible power? For this force is the architect and origina-

tor of you and me, and the entire human race through time, space and existence. I just had a realization...by writing this book, I too am saying "Yes."

2. <u>Reflection.</u> This work will require some psychic space for introspection, self-analysis and reflection.

3. <u>Love.</u> This is the foundational principle from which all good things flow. Love is that energizing ball of light that set forth the good, the beautiful and spectacular in our lives. Love is a mighty power.

4. <u>Forgiveness.</u> You must forgive yourself and others along the way. This letting go, shedding and releasing provides the ultimate freedom for your good to come forth. Forgiveness takes you out of the prison of stagnation and pain, and makes way for the realization that we have all come short of the glory of good. Forgiveness allows you to step into your good and move forward.

5. <u>Participation.</u> This is the last item I will ask you to pack for now, as we must get started; the day is far spent, no more time for procastination, LET'S GO!

Chapter 1

MY DREAM JOURNEY

I am a dreamer. It is believed that we all are. I however, connected to my dreams as a young child and discovered my dream patterns. My mother did not teach me how to make this connection but was very instrumental in giving me a framework and establishing the environment for it to develop. My mother was a Pentecostal Evangelist and so were her father, brother, sister, cousins and a host of other family and friends. I grew up in a family, especially on my mother's side, that believed that God speaks through dreams and visions. For them, dreams were a sort of antenna, a direct hook up, if you will, with the Divine. I remember listening to my mother and her church friends talk about their dreams and what the Spirit had revealed to them. As a result of this, I developed a comfort zone in the dream arena. I did not strain or force the dreams away, as they came naturally and spontaneously in this environment.

Precognitive Dreams

One of my first and very real recognitions of a precognitive dream, (which is having knowledge of an occurrence before it happens) was around the age of ten. One night I had a dream about one of my mother's friends that I had not seen in a while. The next day, I saw her sitting at a bus stop while I was on my school bus. I pondered this seeming coincidence and this was the very first time I actually was conscious of pairing a dream experience. As I reflect on my dreams, at this time, there were also glimpses into the future even before that. As early as kindergarten, I would dream of what we would have the next day for meals and snacks. I was also able to manifest the things I wanted. Perhaps I was sending a subtle message to the cooks and meal planners. Maybe that is what it means to dream until your dreams come true. We can actually get what we want by dreaming about it.

Developmental Dreams

Dreams are affected by your stage in life and your developmental level. For example, when I was a child, I dreamed about things a child would want, mostly food and drink and toys, all of which I could manifest through my dream life. Along those lines, I would dream of the location I would find the money to buy the things I wanted. Spirit, or super consciousness would direct me in my dreams to look on the ground, run an errand for someone, look in the garage, or ask a family member. While I believe we dream primarily within the scope of our spiritual, psychological and intellectual developmental levels, these areas can be increased in your dream life.

You can actually develop and grow in your dreams. Your dreams can actually become your teacher. As a professor, I cannot count the times that new theories, concepts, and ideas have been revealed to me in my dreams. The subconscious never sleeps. We have the capacity to program our subconscious while we sleep and give an assignment, a task, a desire, a problem and to allow it to work. Turn it over to your dreams and let that part of your existence work it out. How many times have you said or heard someone say "Let me sleep on it." This is more than an offhand comment. It actually works if we work it. We can be more adept in our dreams however by having some idea of what we want, so that we can achieve the desired outcome.

Communication Dreams

My Godfather and Godmother, The Reddings died before I turned 12 years old. They loved each other very much. I enjoyed spending time at their home because there was so much love in that house. They were kind and caring with each other. I would listen to the way they talked to each other, touch each other and the wonderful rapport they had with each other. My Godmother made a beautiful home with lovely art and exotic furnishings. This was rare for Black people in the 1950's & 1960's in my circle. I felt privileged to be there in the mist of that beauty in the mist of that love. My Godfather died first. This devastated my Godmother and a part of her died with him. I watched her physically die within that same year. She loved me, but her love for me was not strong enough to hold her to this life. She did, however, come to me in my dreams to soothe and comfort me during that period of time and actually helped me adjust to her not being with me on the physical plane. She would appear in my dreams in a very tranquil and peaceful state. She would smile at me in my dreams and she made me feel loved and that she was with me.

Dreams then can help us contact and communicate with deceased friends and family if that is desired or necessary. Some Hispanics and Native Americans believe you can meet your ancestors and other relatives in your dream world and receive messages from them. I remember vividly having an encounter with a deceased ex-boyfriend in a dream. His name was Jeff and attended college with me in Miami. I loved him so much. I think he was my first true love. We had great fun together. He was tall, dark and handsome. Smooth and cool are the best words to describe him. He was, however, a ladies man. This was a cause for his early demise, for his ex-wife murdered him as he tried to break in her house uninvited. We had lost touch for several years, but we reconnected just before his death. He said to me these words, "I feel about you like Chicken George [in the movie "Roots"] felt about his lover; you are going to always be my woman" One week later he was dead, but the relationship was not over. He made several contacts with me in my dreams. The main contact was in a dream that we had a day and night out on the town together in his blue sports car. He ended our dream date by telling me how much he enjoyed the time we spent together and gave me his telephone number, as he departed. I wish I would have written it down or remembered it. Perhaps that number had some significance. There have been accounts of deceased family member giving their love ones lucky numbers in their dreams.

Directive Dreams

While dreams can help us communicate with those who have transitioned, they can also help direct the living. One such instance occurred in Miami when I was a young woman of about 20. At that time, I was sometimes lost and on the edge, but my mother's dreams warned her when I was going too far. I got a call from my mother and she said to me, "Phyllis are you alright? I had a dream about you and you need to go to church, baby." I told her I was all right, but I knew I was not living right. She gave me the name of a church, Cohen's Temple Church of God in Christ, and asked me to visit. The minister's topic on the day I visited was entitled the "The Spiritual Dropout." I was raised in the Pentecostal and Baptist traditions but wasn't feeling too holy at the time. I was certainly, as the preacher noted, a "Spiritual Drop Out." My mother's dreams brought me back to my spiritual foundation and I believed it saved my life.

There was a woman I met at that church who had a tremendous impact on me. Her name is Queen Esther Hopkins. She too, dreamed dreams, had visions and spoke to God. She was there to direct and help me organize and structure my life. She was an important guide and teacher and her association with me helped to shape my teaching career, because teaching is not just a career it is a calling, an art, a mission, a spiritual thing. She taught me about the power of love, the power of good and the power of God and reminded me that the spirit speaks in dreams. She had a dream that described the family that I would have, when no family was in sight. She had a dream of a repeating temptation that I had and suggested that I stay away. She held me in the light through her dreams. For her dreams warned me, informed me and helped me to become more patient as I waited for the various manifestations of our dreams to come forth. She was also very instrumental in stimulating my psychic dreams by calling me into consistent worship, prayer, and fasting. These three factors caused my dream life to shift to a higher and more profound level. I sincerely believe there is a connection between these powerful forces and a vital dream life; at least it was for me.

So I began fasting, praying, and becoming spiritually attuned and the dreams were coming, and coming and coming. Then, I get a message in a dream that my father made his transition, but this one was expected, as he was old and sick. Then I had a dream that a young, vital man died who I knew just casually as the director of a local community center. This one captured my attention. I was not expecting him to die, nor my Aunt Inell. My Aunt Inell was more than an aunt to me; she was my second mother; she was my mother's youngest sister, who for a period of years lived with us. In this dream there were no visuals, this was an auditory dream, only my mother's voice was present, saying: "Your Aunt Inell is DEAD." That dream woke me up! I prayed for this not to happen, Woe! I did not like this one at all. I called my sister after having this dream and informed her of the dream. She pretty much dismissed the dream as something from nowhere. However it served as a warning, a preparation, a time of adjustment for me, for about five days later my mother called to informed me my Aunt Inell had a brain aneurysm while conducting her women's day celebration and was then unconscious. Two days later my mother called and said "Your Aunt Inell is DEAD."

After that event, I turned my precognitive dreams off. I took the position that I did not want to know, too much responsibility, too much potential pain and, surprisingly, they did stop. For a while, anyway. "Ask and it shall be given" You do have that option to turn down the frequency, but you also have the option to turn it up again if you desire so don't get freaked out. You can handle this and your subconscious is respectful and accommodating. My sister, Norma, was very blunt when she said that if you ever dream anything about me "Don't tell me." I recounted this story to one of my classes and asked them, "Would you want to know if someone had a dream like that about you? I was surprised. The class was split in half. I thought more would say "no." Some said that if they had any wrongs, they wanted to make them right. They wanted an opportunity to take care of any unfinished business, take the trips they always wanted to take, and also some said that they wanted an opportunity to partition spirit on their own behalf to turn things around and to ask for a second chance or more time. Some said that they would like to search out the meaning of the dream. Others took the position of my sister, "I DON'T WANT TO KNOW!" They felt that they would worry about something that may or may not happen. They would rather spend their time enjoying life and not worrying about the end, pointing out that this was something that was out of their control.

Dreams are not all about sad times, dreams can also be about new beginnings. I have seen new friends and lovers in my dreams; I knew they were coming, for I had

met them in my dream life. After meeting them in "real" life
I knew these were relationships I was supposed to cultivate
and develop. I had a dream of being in Italy prior to going,
which stimulated me to buy a ticket and go in the flesh. *Déjà
vu* is a real part of the dream life. You can take a trip, have
an adventure and explore a new universe in your dreams.
Dreaming can assist you to live a fulfilled, interesting and
meaningful life. It is a beautiful world, dreaming can
remind us that we must strive to be happy.

I saw myself leaving my last position as a social work-
er for the state of Florida to become a college professor. I
was prompted in a dream to prepare to leave my last job and
friends and clients, not because I did not like them, but
because there was something else I should do at that time. I
got my resume together; I got my self together and made the
necessary moves. Your mission, your career, your purpose
can be revealed in your dreams. Sometimes I will see
myself flying or standing on the top of a mountain, or meeting with a prophet. This dream is a signal for me to go higher, to leave my fears and apprehensions behind and fly.
Dreams can help you step into your moment. And step into
these spaces with confidence, grace and purpose.

When I am stressed and depressed I turn to my sleep
and dream states for respite, reconciliation, and guidance. It
is in our dream state that we can gain relief from psychological tension. Some of our tension comes from fatigue and
some of our tension results from not having enough to do.
We <u>can</u> find the correct formula... the psychological keys
for restoration of balance. In our sleep we may be directed
to release the problem to the Great Spirit. Many times we
can receive a psychological, physical and spiritual healing in

our dreams and are directed to some book, some place, some
movie, some activity, or someone. Many times we are
directed back to ourselves, and we are reminded that we
have been touched by the light of divinity and awe and are
ultimately immortal beings, for nothing can harm, nor can
hurt us, for we are children of the most high. Therefore,
fear, worry, depression, and anxiety are unnecessary.

During our sleep and dream time we are able to com-
mune with that presence who knows all things, that is
omnipresent, (everywhere at the same time) omnipotent, or
all powerful. Omniscient or all knowing. There is nothing
to fear but fear itself. This knowing again, can be made
clear and revealed in our dreamtime. When in the quiet
serenity of our dreams we find our way back to spirit, to rest,
to wholeness. In truth we are whole, prefect and complete.
Our dreams can direct us there, for in the unconscious realm
we come face to face with ourselves, with others and with
spirit, for we are all one. In your dreams you have the ability to use focus, attention, faith, and will. To utilize this
methodology, I will describe it as a process of going into the
dream and performing a reconstructive dream surgery on
yourself. The mind and spirit is powerful. You have the
ability to perform this operation or procedure. Use the following prescription for your dream therapy to cultivate your
belief!

1. VISUALIZE –See yourself doing the things you
want and the things that give your life meaning, joy and
peace. Structure your life the way that you want it to be.
Put your life, mind, and activities within divine order.
Collect those broken pieces, put them together like a giant
puzzle. Some things have to be reassembled. You can do it

by using the power of visualization. In so doing, you can glimpse into divine mind and see those aspects of self that need work and realignment.

2. PROJECT- Projection is the step beyond visualization. Be the person you want to be; feel the way you want to feel. Feelings can be a great guide for letting us know that something is out of control, out of order, not working for us. We, however, must not make feelings our master. Dreaming is a way to give feelings it rightful place. It is a tool for analysis, our feelings are not who we are, for we are much more than a feeling or impulse. The big self is seated over there and saying come on; it is time to move beyond this nagging feeling or depression. Again, you meet the true self in your dreams.

3. REJECT- During the dreaming process, you have the ability to reject or cancel the aspects of your life that you do not want any more such as behaviors, moods, attitudes, feelings, and relationships.

4. ACCEPT- The acceptance stage is a glorious one. On the acceptance level you have sealed the deal, you have said yes to the possibility of going to this place that lies within yourself and are now ready for the final stage of transformation.

5. TRANSFORMATION- This method is shifting from old to new. You are standing on the mountain of change, the landscape looks magnificent, the horizon is clear and the vista is beautiful. It is like a blood transfusion for this is the ultimate transformation... for old things have passed away, behold all things are made new. You have made a new step.

Walk in the light!

I have provided you with parts of the anatomy of my dreams and a methodology for your own personal exploration. Please remember that your truth lies within you. Dreaming is one method for unraveling the chaos and uncertainty within us and provides REVELATIONS of hope, knowing, beauty, purpose and love. It is now time to listen my friends. Listen to your unconscious. Listen to your heart for flesh and blood has not revealed these things for they come from a part of us that cannot be touched by human hand. It cannot to bought or sold but given only by divine knowledge, intercession and intervention. If this resonates with you, read on.

**"IN A VERY CURIOUS WAY A DREAM TEACHES
US HOW EASILY OUR SOUL IS CAPABLE OF
PENETRATING EVERY OBJECT WHILE
AT THE SAME TIME BECOMING THE OBJECT"**

Novaliss

Chapter 2

DREAMS: AN OVERVIEW

Common Dreams

The following dreams according to psychologists and dream experts occur more frequently than any other dreams.

Falling- Is generally recognized as a symbol of insecurity and a need to build and cultivate confidence and strength.

Being Chased- This is a sign to face your fears.

Death- Symbolizes that a loss or change of some type is at hand. It could be an actual death or a certain aspect of a person dying or transitioning.

Teeth Falling Out- Signifies anxiety, and for me is

a preparation dream to deal with an area of stress and unpleasantness. This dream is usually not viewed in a positive dream context.

Eyes- are the window to the soul and are reflective of mental and spiritual states of mind. This dream usually represents high spiritual and mental elevations, especially when the eyes are bright and illuminated in the dream.

Nudity- Is usually the ability to see through a person's defenses and social masks.

Loss of Hair - Hair falling out is an anxiety dream for some and for others a need to denounce something or change some aspect of your life. It is a sign or a need for letting go.

Isolated Places - This is generally viewed as a need for solitude, reflection and contemplation.

Flying- is a high state of elevation or moving to a higher level in consciousness. (Fontana)

Dreams have intrigued many people and cultures; many indigenous cultures often viewed dreams as messages from God. Especially provocative are those inescapable and compelling "Big Dreams." This concept of the Big Dream was given to us by the Native Americans. They felt that "Big Dreams" have very special and important meanings that should be paid attention to, worked with and addressed. These dreams are usually clear, emotionally charged and speak to you on very deep levels." These questions often arise: Are dreams a source of deep hidden knowledge, to be likened to a sort of sixth sense? Are they random meaningless data, composed of images, thoughts and insignificant garbage that one collects and later discards during the night? Do dreams have any relevance to real life? These are some of the many questions asked.

This work upholds the position that dreams can be a bridge to understanding one's life and affairs. Additionally, dreaming can be a powerful and accessible link to the unconscious level of mind or spiritual domains of existence. This type of linkage is only possible when one understands the principles and possibilities available to them. It is vital that this type of realization and clarity is made on an individual or personal realm first and foremost. This is possible through experimentation, faith, remembering and by the establishment of an understanding of your own dream language. It is important to be able to interpret and become bilingual and conversant with this method of communication. This language is "Soul" language and can only be understood if one is in tuned.

Dreams can and have been useful in a number of ways and serves the following purpose. Dreams Can:

1. Bring messages from the spiritual domain of existence.

2. Provide knowledge of future events.

3. Signal a need for change or needed development.

4. Provide access to creativity and potential and a way to contact the intuitive level of mind.

5. Inspire and encourage.
6. Allow one to find meaning,

purpose and mission in life and open
a window into divine mind and
consciouness.

7.   Provide warnings.

8.   Encourage healing and curative
       methods.

9.   Lead us into psychological and
       spiritual integration.

10.   Encourage us to vent, release, and sublimate
       frustration, anger and aggression.

11.   Direct, instruct and guide.

12.   Enable us to contact others, and
       for others to contact us.

13.   Allow for adventures and fun.

Scientists are now telling us that up to one third of
our lives can have some relevance to our dreams. The key
variables are:

1. How does one access the dream to explore this inward
    journey?
2. What is the formula for decoding the dream?
3. How does one understand the interlocking relationships
of our waking and dreaming lives?
4. How does one log into and become sensitive to the
"force field" that informs all material and non material

essence.

The answers to these questions can be explored in a number of ways. One is through a historical, psychological, and sociological study of various cultural views and experiences. Dreams and dreaming is a topic that has interested some, fascinated others and provided sound guidance and information to many throughout the ages. World cultures have long understood the significance of sleep and dreams. The ancient Greeks and Egyptians erected temples and shrines dedicated to sleep and dreaming. They viewed these temples as healing centers and, as a result, their sick would sleep there because it was believed so deeply that healing or a healing solution could be obtained through dreaming. At these center, some would be guided by priests in prayers and various ritual procedures such as invocations, chants, water healings, purification baths, herbal methods, and periods of fasting.

In India, it was felt that prophetic dreams came to those who had made significant advancement in their soul or spiritual development. The Chinese felt that something deeply mystical occurred during sleep and held a belief that the soul travels to other worlds and dimensions during sleep. Dreams are mentioned in the old and new testaments. According to Judeo-Christian beliefs this is a method of how God speaks to man. In the Buddhist tradition, it is felt that dreams can show you your faults as well as your sins.

Native Americans were so invested in dreaming that they constructed "Dream Catchers" to hold and retain the dream. In the country side of Haiti, a topic of conversation is "What Did You Dream Last Night"? Many events have been foretold in a dream. Take, for example, the sinking of the Titanic, the assassination of President Abraham Lincoln, the death of Tupac Shakur, Hannibal's epic journey. Countless other events were given in dreams prior to their occurrences.

The natural and social sciences can be useful in understanding and appreciating dreams. Psychologically speaking, Sigmund Freud's Psychoanalytical theory is partially based on Dream Analysis. For Freud, dreams provide a storehouse of information as they deal with and reflect a person's psychological issues and history. Carl Jung thought that dreams were essential as well and a methodology to tap into the "Collective Unconscious," that vast universal storehouse of knowledge. Nathanial Kleitman and Eugene Aserinsky felt that dreams were so important, that they started the first Dream Laboratories, so that dreams could be studied clinically and scientifically. Most scientists believe that one dreams during the REM stage. (Rapid Eye Movement) Some dream specialists believe that all mammals dream, and hold that for newborn babies' dreams are probably their first language. Many who are around newborns observe them smiling and demonstrating a variety of behaviors during the REM stage.

Dreaming involves stillness and a certain level or relaxation. When the brain waves begin to drop to the Alpha stage, one begins to benefit from the release of healing and reinvigorating hormones. During this stage, scientists believe that one begins to shift in and out of consciousness. The next drop is into the Theta stage, and most experts believe that it is this stage that most people dream. The final stage is the Delta stage, which is even a deeper level of relaxation. During this stage it is believed that one does not dream but the body is so still and relaxed it allows itself to be repaired and regenerated. Relaxation tends to be a major ingredient in dreaming, then healing and intuition can follow.

Another way to access the dream is ones "Intentionality." Inherent in the intention, is faith. One's belief system tends to set the parameters for the experience. With this component intact one can began to program the subconscious mind to first remember the dream, and then begin to put this level of consciousness to work on your behalf by beginning to ask it questions and allow it to engage in problem solving. Knowing the right questions to ask becomes very important to obtaining the right answer. This implies that one must be somewhat self aware. Psychologists hold that prophetic dreamers tend to have a higher I.Q. This realm is not for amateurs but holds that one should bring something to the "dreaming table" for it to work for you.

As one becomes conversant with their dreams an ongoing dialogue can be established. This can be done through journaling, letter writing, or discussing your dream with a "Dreaming Buddy" or support group. This developing and ongoing relationship with youself can be one of the most rewarding relationships ever. One way to become conversant with your dreams is to understand your patterns. It is imperative that you can retrace the dream. What was the emotion, sensation, imagery, parallel, and synchronicity? Can you pair the experience? Were there any relationships established? Did the dream become actualized or true on some level? These are some of the parameters to use in prophetic dreaming. The conscious and subconscious minds must meet. How many times have you been dreaming and you get a message from the conscious mind that you need to go to the bathroom, or wake up for other reasons. You sent your subconscious mind back a message: "Not yet!" Or you speed up the dream, or put it on "pause." This relationship with both levels of mind is possible, and operational in many cases.

To make the best of your dreaming potential you may consider engaging in the following:

1. Prepare yourself by clearing and cleaning your mind, body and spirit. Facilitate your space by making it as comfortable and relaxing as possible. If there are any wrongs you have done or been done by others, forgive.

2. Relax yourself, be still, be quite, still yourself to receive and hear from the deep communications of your soul.

3. Utilize your spiritual attributes: Have faith, be patient, love and honor your creator, yourself and others.

4. Be grateful that this opportunity is available to you. Gratitude opens one up to receive more, and more and more, until your cup overflows with bounty.

5. If you have a particular problem or question ask for the answer: "Seek and you shall find, knock and the door will be opened for you."

6. Pay attention to your attention, take notice of the clues or answers given in your dreams.

7. Record your messages: This can be recorded in print or you may use of any technology you find useful.

8. Enjoy yourself: Dreaming is a privilege and a divine opportunity. Enjoy your journey and your life!

Sleep and Dreams

Sleep is the gateway into our dream life, and as a result is very important to the dreaming process and our overall health. For most people sleep is a pleasurable experience. Many of us after a busy day cannot wait to get some sleep, to shut down, rest and are free from responsibilities. Shakespeare once referred to sleep as "the death of each day's life."

Human beings spend about a third of their lives sleeping. Most people are sleepiest between the hours of 1 and 4 am. We are diurnal creatures, meaning that we are active during the daylight hours and sleep at night. We do have our individual biorhythms, however, as this is evident by what we refer to as the night people who prefer a reverse schedule. We are more productive during our most preferred time of the day. Some people experience a sleepy period in mid afternoon; as a result, in many countries people take a siesta, or a nap in the afternoon. We spend on an average of about eight hours a night sleeping and about ninety minutes per night dreaming (Carskadon, 1993; Dement & Vaughan, 1999).

In the 1950's, three scientists collaborated to do the groundbreaking experiments on sleep and the sleeping process. They offer and explain five distinct stages of sleep. These early pioneers were Nathaniel Kleitman, Eugene

Arerinksy, and William Dement. We are deeply indebted to these individuals for giving us the language and the tools for discussing and understanding the sleeping process. They were also instrumental in setting up the first sleep laboratories where electrodes were connected to the scalp of the persons being studied. These electrodes recorded brain-wave activity during sleep and dreaming and rapid eye movement (REM). Scientists believe we do our most active dreaming during this stage. Kleitman, Arerinksy and Dement identified the following stages of dreams:

Stage 1 - Breathing slows down, the mind relaxes and you began to feel drowsy. The brain patterns are more in the Alpha State or the stage of relaxation, the blood pressure and heart rate drops. After about 10 minutes in this stage you move into stage two.

Stage 2 - During this stage, you become progressively more relaxed and are less easily disturbed. If there is noise in another room your brain will register a response but you are not likely to wake up. After about twenty minutes in this level you fall into the deepest level of sleep stages 3 and 4.

Stages 3 and 4 – It is difficult to distinguish these two, as they vary only in degrees, both are marked as being in the delta level, and you are out like a light.

Stage 5 - In REM sleep you are internally active but physically paralyzed. The eyelids are shut but the eyeball more back and forth frantically. REM dreams are believed to be more vivid, visual and detailed.

Sleep again is important to our overall health and well-being. Many, who are sleep deprived, experience paranoia, hallucinations, lack concentration, experience memory loss, and slurred speech. All aspects of the physical, emotional and mental health are compromised. Sleep helps conserve energy and allows for restoration and rejuvenation. It recharges our batteries.
(Kassin)

"IF WE MEDITATE ON A DREAM SUFFICIENTLY LONG AND THOROUGHLY-IF WE TAKE IT ABOUT WITH US AND TURN IT OVER AND OVER-SOMETHING ALMOST ALWAYS COMES OF IT."

CARL JUNG

Chapter 3

THE CARL JUNG FACTOR

"Dreams Do Not Deceive, They Do Not Lie, They Do Not Distort Or Disguise. They Are Invariably Seeking To Express Something That the Ego Does Not Know and Does Not Understand"
Carl Jung

The work of Psychologist Carl Jung has been my greatest theoretical inspiration. His classic contribution *Man and His Symbols* owes its existence to one of his own dreams where his work was shared for public consumption, rather than an elite psychological audience. In this book, he takes us into the realm of the unconscious, using dreams as a primary methodology.

Jung defines a dream by writing, "Dreams are a normal psychic phenomenon that transmits unconscious reactions or spontaneous impulses to the consciousness" (Jung, 1964, p.5).

For Jung dreams are a real part of us and can serve as an excellent guide or guru through the unconscious realms of mind. Through dreaming, we are able to establish a relationship between the conscious and subconscious mind. Dreams can help us break through the barriers of the unknown and bring into focus those things that keep us in turmoil. Dreams can lead us into the beauty of self-knowledge and self-fulfillment.

Jung clearly did not believe that dreams were random or chance events, but as real as anything else related to the individual. He suggested that man does not fully perceive his reality for it is many times clouded under surface phenomena. Major aspects of us are vague, hidden and unknown. He theorized that with the aid of dream analysis one can penetrate the unconscious, so the self can be illuminated, reviewed and utilized for self understanding and growth.

Jung was greatly influenced by the legendary and inescapable psychologist Sigmund Freud, whose primary therapeutic focus deviled within the unconscious realms. "Psychology is an attempt to deal with the workings of the unconscious" (Jung, 1964.) From a psychological perspective the purpose of dreams is to restore our psychological balance by revealing our drives, instincts, impulses, fears and wishes. Freud's ground breaking contribution and treatise on psychoanalysis, which was his methodology for examining the unconscious realms of the mind, proposed dream analysis and free association as mechanisms for this examination. For Freud "Human Behavior is just the tip of the iceberg." His central focus was what lies beneath, what is behind the veil or the behavior, what motivates men and women, boys and girls to think, believe, and act. For Freud, it was unconscious forces that have been suppressed and hidden from view.

Through dream analysis, one can place a spotlight on these aspects and trace the dots back to the problem, and to the self. As a result, the unconscious motives can be illuminated, and resolution can be fostered. For Freud, human beings are a complex energy system that can be volatile, passive, destructive, fragile, powerful, confused but capable of transcending some of the chaos and void in their lives. This psychic energy needs to be understood and sublimated, and reconciled before harmony can be restored. Jung again, was greatly affected by Freud and his great mind. It has been said that Freud was the greatest mind that has ever lived. What a compliment. What respect. More will be said about Freud and his views on dreams.

For me, Jung took the notion of dreams further by connecting dreams to "The Collective Unconsciousness" universal mind, ultimate intelligence or that vast storehouse of information and knowledge that is our history, our present and our future. Jung holds that dreams can lead us to individualization and wholeness by overcoming fragmentation. He states that self-control is rare, largely because of dissociation, unchecked emotions and because large areas of the mind remain in darkness. Jung holds that self control is a civilizing process and invites us to engage a space for the civilized being. His writings elicit important questions:

1. Do we know all there is to know about our
   selves?

2. Is there a mystical participation in the universe?

3. Do we have an unconscious intent with someone or some
   thing else?

4. Can we synthesize the individual psyche?

Jung made the statement that "Dreams can give yourself a way." The answer, my friend, may be hidden in a dream.

Dreams are a great starting point for this type of investigation through the self. Jung believed you can begin anywhere such as with …

An inspired writing

Meditation

By focusing on an object or situation

Art

Casual conversations

Jung asserted that man's faculty to produce symbols is most basic when dreamimg. Dreams have a purposeful structure and include our secret thoughts. He thought that clarity fluctuates "just beyond the threshold of recall." The consciousness can only hold so much information; other information is stored in the unconscious. The question is "Can we recall or recover that information"? Self-recovery, in many cases, relies on being able to remember. The conscious also represses information that it finds too difficult or painful to handle. Because of this, Jung felt that "Hysterical symptoms can be seen in just about all normal persons." For Jung, there are pathologically disturbances that lie within.

Jung is remembered for offering the Seven Major Archetypes as aspects of ourselves that appear in our dreams. They are as follows:

The Wise Old Man- This archetype can also be presented as a woman and was called the mana personality. It is a primal source of vitality and growth that can heal but also damage. The wise old man may appear as a professor, priest, and sometimes a teacher. It is quasi-divine and can be used to lead one towards or away from the higher levels of development. Jung, himself, had a long relationship with this archetype, which he calls Philemon.

The Trickster- The Trickster is full of tricks, jokes and pranks and may appear in dreams as a clown or sinister figure. The trickster is overly playful to the point that he or she can interrupt and spoil pleasure in dreams, it is a master game player and the trickters are known to be disruptive, untamed and antisocial.

The Persona- The Persona is the mask that we have reconciled ourselves to and can be very dangerous if identified with too much. This is the self that we present to the outside world. To be naked in a dream generally means we have lost the persona.

The Shadow- The Shadow represents the dark side and Jung gave Freud credit for introducing what is referred to as the "abyss of human nature." The shadow is brutal, selfish and uncivilized and arouses feelings of fear and anguish. This part of the personality cannot fully be disguised and must be tamed, integrated and harmonized into the personality.

The Divine Child- The Divine Child represents the true self that includes innocence and vulnerability. It generally appears as a baby or infant and can put the ego back in place because the child humbles the self, and helps to negate arrogance and narcissism from the personality.

The Anima and Animus- Animus represents the masculine aspects and qualities of being and the Anima represents the feminine qualities. Jung asserted that both aspects are within and lead to fully exploring what is generally unexplored. If not recognized it can lead to a stymied human potential or to over-emotionalism or ruthlessness and destruction.

The Great Mother- The Great Mother plays a pivotal role in spiritual development. She is earthy yet divine and embodies feminine mystery and power. She is fierce and nurturing, gentle, yet strong. She serves to assist in psychological integration and development. The Great Mother is also a protector, for she watches over and a cares for the child.

Jung brilliantly captures these aspects of ourselves as they appear as characters and messengers for self acknowledgment and development. Jung takes a leap into the metaphysical when he states that dreams originate in a spirit that is not human. He accounts that early men and women were guided and directed by their instincts and their dreams. He made what some consider a startling and illuminated comment when he said, "Moses and other prophets when they said they spoke with God, were in affect saying they heard voices…were they hallucinating? Or having a profound encounter with the "All?" Modern Psychology would hold that these people were psychotic human beings. Others believe that God spoke to these "Special" people then, but refuses to speak with us now. We are very confused!

Dreaming can help to regain composure and to remarry or rejoin the self. Jung reminds the dreamer to be "prepared to be confronted." We must also remember that the healing process comes out of the individual; no one can impose growth upon another. That person must agree to be engaged. Keep in mind that introspection and self knowledge is the goal.

"ALL THAT WE SEE OR SEEM IS BUT A DREAM WITHIN A DREAM"

Edgar Allan Poe

Chapter 4

STRESS AND THE UNCONSCIOUS

The world today generates stress, depression and confusion. A stressed out person is an overwhelmed person. Stress is an inability or difficulty to adjust and adapt to daily life. Some people are stressed because of too much stimuli and this is defined as hyper stress, while other people are stressed because of too little (Hypo) stress. It is true that many ills are born of boredom, loneliness and a lack of solid discipline. A tremendous number of people are stressed because of psychological tension and a lack of individualization.

Jung coined the term "individualization" and defined it as the conscious coming to terms with one's inner center he called the psychic nucleus. For Jung individualization is possible when the self is discovered. The self, for Jung, is the *inner guiding factor*. This is different from the conscious personality and can only be grasped through the investigation of one's own dreams and the discovery and information that exists in the unconscious realm.

Dreams contain valuable information that can assist in reaching inner growth, integration, and fulfilling one's destiny. This is the greatest human achievement.   Well meaning people are afraid of the unconscious and of psychology and spirituality. Exploring the unconscious through dreams can provide a bridge or link between the conscious and unconscious states of mind. It is recommended that one must become bilingual with dream language and study it as though studying a foreign language... consistently, diligently and practically. We must practice the language.

The purpose of paying attention to one's dreams is to restore psychological balance. Jung felt that not only must fragmentation be overcome, but also the shadow. The shadow is described as the worse side of a person's nature. The shadow is the dark side of the psyche; it contains egoism, mental laziness, plots, schemes, carelessness, love of money and possessions, evil remarks, fear, and cowardness. Some people feel compelled to live out their worse side, and ultimately it will cause themselves and others pain.

Dream analysis can minimize fragmentation by confrontation and sublimation of the shadow which can lead to the domain of individuation and self actualization. Dreams can move one to the light, for the ego needs clarity, strength, and honest self-examination. Re-organization is a path to the cosmic human being...the best in each of us.

The ultimate goal for the individual is to reach for self realization, integration, selfhood, individualization and wholeness. (Jung)

DREAMS ARE SUCCESSION OF IMAGES, WHOSE
FUNCTION IS TO REDUCE ANXIETY AND TEN-
SION BY BRINGING BACK MEMORIES OF THE
PAST THAT IN SOME WAY IS ASSOCIATED WITH
OUR FEARS, DRIVES AND GRATIFICATION"

Sigmund Freud

Chapter 5

SIGMUND FREUD'S CONTRIBUTION TO THE STUDY OF DREAMS

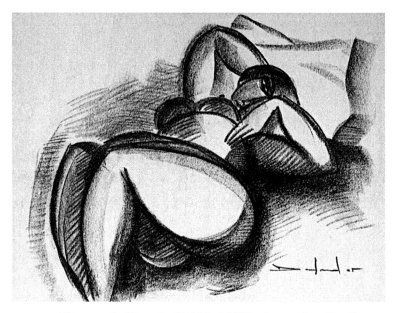

Sigmund Freud (1856-1939) born in Freiberg, Moravia and died in London, England has been distinguished as one of the greatest thinkers that the world has every known. This extraordinary visionary and innovator left his mark extensively in the psychological area.

Freud published the book *The Interpretation of Dreams* in 1899. By then he was in his mid forties. Freud was also trained as a neurologist and had an interest in the causes of neurosis in the unconscious state of mind. Freud, himself, went through self-analysis and was convinced that dreams play a great role in providing access to deep inner understanding. He believed that most dreams were repressed ideas or simply wish fulfillments. He felt that our deepest urges become more manageable through dreaming, as they serve as a key to the unconscious mind. (Fontana, 1991)

Dream analysis is one of a two-layer approach (the other is called free-association) for uncovering unresolved psychological tension. This therapeutic approach is called Psychoanalysis, of which Sigmund Freud is the father and foremost pioneer. Freud felt that dreams have two primary contents. One is called the Latent Content, which has coded symbolism and is what the unconscious reveals, and the second is called the Manifest Content, which is a clearer picture of what is going on and is a reflection of the conscious mind. His study and articulation in the arena of dreams have been foundational and central to dream interpretation. In his view, the mind has three primary structures:

1. The ego or "I" which is self conscious and self-aware. It controls the conscious mind. This part of the mind has a will and is relatively rational.

2. The Preconscious Mind is able to access facts, ideas, memories, and has motive.

3. The Personal Unconscious Mind stores repressed memories, unacknowledged wishes, conflicts, emotions, and urges. This is the part of mind that Freud calls the "Id" which is the instinctual and primitive state of mind.

Freud hypothesized that dreams are coded messages that reflect our expressed fears, impulses, desires, and our unconscious motives. Freud reasoned that through dream analysis these aspects of ourselves can come to the surface so that they can be acknowledged and recognized and ultimately dealt with and resolved. He noted that dreams are a succession of images, whose function is to reduce anxiety and tension by bringing back memories of the past that, in some way, are associated with our fears, drives and gratification. As they relate to wish fulfillment and gratification, dreams are a mental representation of the things we want. Freud felt that people were in a better position of getting that they want, if it was clear to them what they want. In a dream, many times a person cannot distinguish what is real and experience the same emotions, as if they had actually happened. In this regard, the dreamer is able also to experience and it is then possible to work through the emotional and psychological pain. Dreaming can make room for realistic thinking and, therefore, can be a cathartic experience, leading to transparency, emotional synthesis, and a redistribution of psychic energy. (Hall, 1999)

Freud's work on dreams and the role of the unconsciousness has provided much in terms of how we view and interpret the dreaming process and provides a great launching pad for the exploration of dreams. We must acknowledge this mental giant for giving us the vocabulary and a theoretical perspective for exploring something that all cultures, religions, and people do and that is dream. The universal practice and phenomena of dreaming is inescapable and can be a starting place for self-knowledge and self-understanding.

"DREAMS ARE THE EASIEST WAY TO ENTER THE REALM OF THE UNCONSCIOUS"

Edgar Cayce

Chapter 6

THE SLEEPING PROPHET

Edgar Cayce (1877-1945) better known as the sleeping prophet, gave quite a contribution to human society. He was also known as the most well known seerer and prophet in the United States. At an early age, he claimed to have visions and could speak with and see the dead. Born in Hopkinsville, Kentucky and with a very limited formal education, he was still able to glean information from books by sleeping with them under his pillow. Cayce has been able to predict some amazing events in history such as the Great Depression and World Wars I and II. He also spoke of the Holocaust in Europe. Cayce was able to tap into the vast reservoir or knowledge known as the Akashic Record. This is a text that is said to contain the very thoughts and actions of every human being that has ever lived.

"Edgar Cayce taught that dreams were the "safest" way to enter this realm of unconsciousness. He even said that nothing occurs in our outer lives that was not already foreshadowed in our dreams." (Puryear, p.117) He referred to dreams as the gateway to heaven and the house of God. He emphasized that it was imperative to recall the dream to be able to truly benefit from the dream and he recommends the following to assist us in dream recall.
1. Pre-sleep suggestion or auto suggesting to the conscious and subconscious mind to remember the dream.
2. Do not move the body upon awaking to remain in the dream state and position long enough to transfer data.
3. Get the gist of the dream.
4. Use the essence of the dream in life.

Cayce also offers tips of decoding the dream by:
1. Identifying the mood of the dream.
2. Identifying the subject or theme of the dream.
3. Identifying the movement of the dream. (Watch, listen, act, plan, etc.)
4. Identifying the nature of the inner minds activity.

Cayce hypothesized that human beings have a dual nature. It is important that we allocate time each day to each area of our life, both natural and spiritual for balance and wholeness. The soul or spiritual nature of humans require communion with the divine. The personality needs contact with people and the body needs movement and exercise. The mind needs centering and stillness. Cayce offers a number of recommendations for access into this realm of consciousness. Chanting or music raises the cosmic vibration level. Breathing purifies, energizes and clarifies, allowing easier entry into the unconscious. Exercise and movement helps to open our charkras or energy centers located within the body. A straight spine is recommended for a better flow of energy throughout the human structure. Exercise is needed for strengthening the circulation and charging the electric energy in the body. Meditation and prayer are also recommended to open the portals to the divine or the cosmic realm. All aspects of our being need some attention according to Cayce and none of us are totally balanced at all times.

Cayce argued that dreams may be of a physical, mental or spiritual nature and that the soul content of a person may include telepathy, clairvoyance, precognition, communing with deceased relatives, friends, angels, prophets or God. Cayce thought everyone should work with their dreams rather that try to interpret them. Dreams may encourage, reprimand, instruct, inspire, seduce, or guide. Much of how understanding occurs is contingent upon attitude, motivation and attunement. Cayce was of the opinion that information can be received about the health and needs of the body and one can be guided and directed in dreams as a healing method.

Edgar Cayce stressed patience and described patience as another dimension of consciousness, which is extremely important to entering the silence and plugging into the spiritual domain.

THE MAN WHO THINKS HE CAN

IF YOU THINK YOU ARE BEATEN, YOU ARE;
IF YOU THINK YOU DARE NOT, YOU DON'T.
IF YOU LIKE TO WIN, BUT THINK YOU CAN'T
IT IS ALMOST A CINCH YOU WON'T
IF YOU THINK YOU'LL LOSE, YOU'RE LOST,
FOR OUT IN THE WORLD WE FIND
SUCCESS BEGINS WITH A FELLOW'S WILL;
IT'S ALL IN THE STATE OF THE MIND.
IF YOU THINK YOU'RE OUTCLASSED, YOU ARE;
YOU'VE GOT TO BE SURE OF YOURSELF
BEFORE
YOU CAN EVER WIN A PRIZE.
LIFE'S BATTLES DON'T ALWAYS GO
TO THE STRONGER OR FASTER MAN;
BUT SOON OR LATE THE MAN WHO WINS
IS THE MAN WHO THINKS HE CAN

Anita Bell

Chapter 7

PRINCIPLES OF EMPOWERMENT

The following principles may prove helpful in increasing integration in our dream lives. A principled life lends itself to clarity and provides a framework for engaging the individual from a more holistic perspective.

Principle #1 The Law of Purpose

Purpose outlines a destination or a goal to be obtained. It marks a standard to be reached. To have no goal is to have nothing that is tangible or is to have nothing in mind. Purpose is definable and it is solid. Whatever the mind can conceive and believe the mind can achieve. Purpose is what has been conceived or received in your consciousness. It is a mental construct that provides vision and clarity, along with momentum.

What have you conceived for yourself this year, this month, this week, today? What is your purpose? A person who is married to a purpose is unstoppable, for purpose is a formidable force that cannot be denied. Purpose sets in motion and drives divine ideas. We live in a mental and spiritual universe. It is like our ideas have a life unto themselves with a mental consciousness that works on our behalf. These ideas have a motion and energy. Nothing just happens, it happens by cause and effect relationships. Your purpose is your mission. With this in mind, it is vital that we have a mission statement. This statement propels the purpose into the cosmos and gives your purpose force and power.

When purpose has been established, you can call on three other P's to assist you in your efforts:
Planning
Picturing
Projecting

Planning is like calling a play. It sets a design. It provides a framework or strategy. It is helpful when you have a plan to write it down. Writing ideas down is like magic. Planning keeps you on task and allows you to assess your progress over time. Planning also allows you the ability to outline steps in the goal setting process and those things that need to be done in order to complete the task or the desired effect.

Picturing allows you to see yourself winning, achieving and living well. Picturing provides a mental image. Without this visioning, it is difficult to accomplish anything. Many of us think in pictures. We need visuals to assist us. See yourself with the trophy, the degree, the house, healed, happy and psychologically well.

***Principle #2** The Law of Belief*
In order to be an effective dreamer, you have to believe! Belief is a form of faith and faith is the fuel that sustains your purpose. It has holding power! It has staying power. Faith is the security blanket that covers and keeps you… It covers us with protection and provides an invisible shield of power as it firmly implants your missions and goals. Faith freezes and secures your position and at the same time propels you upward toward your goal. Faith, like purpose, is an invaluable ingredient. We need faith for everything we do… to drive, to go to school, to work, to take care of ourselves, to pay our bills, to carry out our responsibilities, to achieve our objectives… we must believe it is possible. Without this belief, many times we stop, give up, or won't even try.

Belief is an essential building block for success. It is divine confidence. Think about it, when a person moves and acts with confidence, this is the kind of person we follow, for we believe this person is going someplace. This person is believable. A confident person embodies a type of cosmic quality that allows them to do amazing things. "As a man believes, so is he."

When we have faith, we cut into an invisible substance and manifest what we want. Faith empowers us to do and have those things we desire. Our faith should be connected to our purpose. This dynamic duo acts as an atomic force and moves on our behalf. It has the ability to sort through and tap into divine mind. With faith everything has its beginning.

On this page, provide three statements of belief. These statements should be closely aligned to your mission statement. This is your affirming statement. For example, I believe I can have healthy relationships. I believe I can complete three courses next semester. Be specific. Name them and claim them.

_____

_____

_____

_____

_____

_____

_____

_____

_____

_____

_____

_____

_____

_____

_____

_____

_____

_____

_____
_____
_____
_____
_____
_____
_____

Principle #3 *The Principle of Work*

Effective dreams should be paired with effective work. Like begets like. Get up! Get out and do something! These words were spoken by the late great Tupac Shakur. We must be willing to work. The question is what have you done lately? Through work we build upon our dreams. I believe that effective work can evoke more and more dreams. We have more dream content when we are active. You probably have heard of the biblical expression that states "Faith without works is dead." There is no exception to the rule or law. In order to get something out you must put something in... That is the law! Sorry folks that is just the way it is. I would like to define work as a divine activity that leads to excellence or goal achievement. Work sets up a cause and effect relationship. Work is the cause... achievement is the effect. It leads us closer to where we want to be.

For many, work is a bad word; it does not have to be; it is all in how you approach it; it is how you take it, and make it. As a matter of fact, work is a good thing. It is how civilizations have been developed, discoveries made, victories won. It is an actualizing activity whereby we get what we want! When we approach work from this perspective, it should energize us. It should give us a special charge. Work

should make us happy because we can actually see ourselves moving closer to our goal. Dreams add to the input
and output of our lives and work provides the needed fuel.

When you work, you are actively participating in
your mission. With this my friend, lets do something positive. On this page, please list the activities you have or will
perform as it relates to accomplishing your mission or purpose.

_____

_____

_____

_____

_____

_____

_____

_____

_____

_____

_____

_____

_____

_____

_____

_____

_____

_____

_____

_____

_____

_____

Principle #4 *The Law of Motivation*

Motivation means to move or to be energized in a given direction. Motivation stimulates and drives the engine. To be motivated is a joyous occasion. It makes the moment bright and light. It is deeply synchronized with the laws of faith, purpose, and work. Motivation is that shot in the hip that gets you going. It is a mental tonic or vitamin to the psyche. It awakens the enthusiasm necessary to initiate and complete a project or goal. It makes taking that first step and subsequent steps easier. "A journey of a thousand miles starts with one step." Motivation minimizes psychological pain and helps to eliminate fear. With motivation, no task is too hard for it equips the person with the zeal and zest necessary to carry out our objectives.

When a person is motivated s/he is able to see the big picture. They are able to visualize the end product. Motivation is your appetizer and dessert. Motivation makes the task more satisfying. Motivation glories itself in the process of motion as well; it is priceless. In this view, you don't have to wait to be happy, you can be happy as you go. You can be happy because you have what it takes. You can be happy and whole because we have all the tools we need to make it happen. A motivated person is a person on fire!

On this page discuss how you motivate yourself and list specific examples of what you where able to achieve while motivated.

_____

_____

_____

_____
_____
_____
_____
_____
_____
_____
_____
_____
_____
_____
_____

Principle #5 *The Law of Giving*

Giving is good for us. What you give, in like fashion will be given unto you. "Give abundantly and you will be rewarded in kind." "Give minimally and you will be rewarded minimally." Karmic forces are at work for it is one of the laws of the universe. The more we plant, the more we grow. Giving can enrich our dreaming life as well.

On August 2, 2006 I learned an important lesson on giving. This is what happened: I was invited to visit Trinidad for the 2006 Emancipation Celebration on August 1, 2006. I stayed in the home of my friend's cousin for a number of days. At the end of my visit, I decided to leave my friend's relative $200.00. I gave another relative $100.00 for taking me to the airport and various places while on the trip. My host insisted that I take the money back and use it for my own benefit, but I did not. I had to make a detour to Grenada and Barbados in route back to Miami to await an open flight. (I traveled on a buddy pass and had little extra cash). On the flight back, there was a folded $100.00 bill in my make up case to help me in the time of my need. That's just how fast this law can work.

On this page recount aspects of your giving and how you beleive you were rewarded for giving.

_____

_____

_____

_____

_____

_____

_____

_____

_____

_____

_____

_____

_____

_____

_____

_____

_____

_____

_____

"ANOTHER NAME FOR A SHAMAN IS A DREAMER"

Chapter 8

HOW TO HEIGHTEN AND GAIN MASTERY OF OUR DREAMING ATTENTION

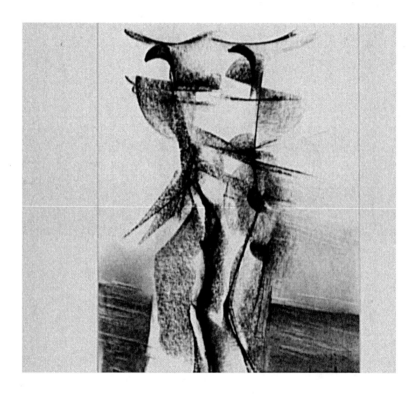

Noted anthropologist and Mystic, Carlos Castaneda in his book *The Art of Dreaming* provides deep insights into the dreaming process from a shamanistic perspective. A Shaman is a person who can go into other worlds and realms of existence and bring back information. In this book, Castaneda tells of how he served as an apprentice with a Mexican Yaqui Indian sorcerer named Don Juan Matus. Matus was a spiritual master also known as a sorcerer in his tradition. Matus taught Castaneda about the role and nature of perception and how it works in shaping our world. Matus held that there is an unseen world around us of ancestors and spiritual forces that can be called upon through practice. He called people, who have the ability to interact with these forces or energies, "Intermediaries."

Matus contended that our world, which we believe to be unique and absolute, is only one in a cluster of consecutive worlds, arranged like the layers of an onion, He asserted that even though we have been energetically conditioned to perceive solely our world, we still have the capability of entering into those other realms, which are as real, unique, absolute, and engulfing as our own world. (Castaneda 1993)

Having the energy to "seize them" and to make them accessible is the task at hand. Matus thought that this was possible through a process he called "energetic conditioning." He held that a practical way to achieve this conditioning is to put dreams to use and he offered a practical guide whereby this can be done. He felt that dreams are a "Gateway to infinity" and other domains of existence. He invited us to take this awesome ride, provided that we are ready and trained to do so.

For Matus, the most important aspect of dreaming is the experiences we encounter. This is not limited to just words, scenes and people but also the actual sensation and the awareness taken from the dream that lives in our bodies and minds. Castaneda came to the conclusion, during his apprenticeship with Matus that "the human psyche is infinitely more complex than our mundane or academic reasoning had led us to believe." There are a myriad of energies that are unavailable to us due to our lack of belief, perception, and psychic energy. Additionally, one must have the ability to make the abstract concrete. This can be achieved through practice and fixations of the mind. We must have "freedom to perceive, without obsessions." (Castaneda p.2) In this domain, there is no compulsion for outside gain.

Matus insisted that the starting point of our investigation into the world of the metaphysical starts with our perception. He holds that this universe is made of energy (first cause). Energy is the common denominator, energy is everything. It must be understood that in the world there are objects, but energy is first, and then objects. For Matus, energy is the essence of the world.

Before one can engage this energy fully, there must be a cultivation of mind. This raises a very important question. How do we cultivate our minds so that our dreams and our lives make sense? This type of cultivation requires the breakdown of barriers of doubt, fear and limitation and of course a realization that we live and have our being in an energy centered, spiritual, multidimensional universe, and that it is accessible and available to us.

Matus also believed in the importance of having a spiritual guide. He called his own "Nagual." This concept refers to any person, male or female, who possesses a specific kind of energy configuration, which to a seer appears as a double luminous ball. Seers believe that when one of these persons enters into the sorcerers' world that extra load of energy is turned into a measure of strength and the capacity for leadership. Thus, the Nagual is the natural guide, the leader of a party of sorcerers. (Castaneda 1993) These are people who are keenly aware of energy currents and can sense, interact, bend, reshape energy through the power of mind, memory and intention. You must also learn to ride the waves of energy, like a surfer rides the wave of water in the ocean.

According to Matus there are a number of actions you can take to build up your dream body.

1. You must set up the dream. In the setting up process you must stay with the theme of the dream and don't let it go; don't jump around from place to place. Focus on something specific. Concentration, integrity, serious- ness and focus are required. In training and assisting in these areas Matus request, "In your dreams tonight you must look at your hand." In other words, you must pay close attention and looking at your hands tonight will require your focused attention and ener- gy, but don't worry, you have energy in reserve. During the dream process look around closely, take glances, listen attentive- ly. This is exercising the dreaming attention.

2. The second step is centered on energy re- employment. Dreaming is an energy-gener- ating process. What is important during this stage is that we lose self-importance. We must humble ourselves and release the ego. Self importance becomes a block and hin-

drance to the dreaming processes. According to Matus," most of our energy goes to upholding our importance." In this stage, we need control, don't get hung up on the dream, let it go. Don't get bogged down. Now you can use one dream to trigger another dream. In this stage, you are able to interact with what Matus terms inorganic beings. He cautions, however, not to call on them until you are ready. Fear is a great indicator that you are not ready. If you encounter fear, ask them to come back when you have more power or strength. He feels that these inorganic beings have the potential to be allies, friends and guides. They can also scare and frighten you if you are not ready for the encounter. As you move forward during this stage, they will began to speak to you, to give you answers to questions that you may have. They will talk to you about things that are penitent to this world, and guide you step by step, to help you transcend the limited understanding and vistas of the human mind and transport you into others worlds and experiences, into the realm of pure spirit. After the relationship with the inorganic beings have been established, judgment must be suspended and allow them to come. When they are truly allies, they have the ability to teach, instruct and take you places beyond your ability to imagine, for they exist within the domain of the infinite, the limitless, and the possible.

The following is recommended to assist and aid in facilitating the dreaming process:

    A.   Turn off the internal dialogue
    B.   Wear a gold ring on your finger or, headband, or tight belt or necklace as forms of grounding. They can act as skin centers to keep you in contact with your natural body.
    C.   Keep your skin clean and free from debris and oils.
    D.   Quartz crystals are useful as energy producers and can be used on or near the body
    E.   Falling asleep in total silence gives you a better entry into the dream world.

3.   "The third gate of dreaming is reached when you find yourself in a dream, staring at someone else that is asleep, and that someone else turns out to be you." (Castaneda, 1993. p141) It is important that you move around during this stage to keep the body fluid and in touch with itself. It is during this stage that the dreaming body begins to merge with the physical body. During this stage, you should be able to see and sense energy. According to Matus, "Dreamers have a rule of thumb... they see energy every time they gaze at an item in the daily world. In dreams, if they see the energy of an item, they know they are dealing with a real world no matter how dis-

torted that world may appear to their dreaming attention."

During Castaneda's study in Mexico, he had various experiences and dreams. One particular dream he shared with a woman at a church. She taught him how to project his intentions in his dreams. Practice for this activity is a process called glazing, where one looks at an object and memorizes every detail, watch everything, and is super alert. Once this is achieved, through the process of memory, recall the object in detail without looking at it. In your dreams, you are able to visualize what you want and react to the vision in your dreams. This is a process of creation and recreation. He was also instructed to point at what interested him with his little finger and could also yell in his dreams, as points of instruction for developing clarity in his dreams.

One of the most stunning aspects of Matus' experience in dreaming, for me, is that we have the ability to created alternate possibilities though intentional visioning in our dreams and become a creator of our realities. These experiences changed Castaneda completely and amplified his dream training tremendously. It is so exciting; it is food for thought, and a methodology and a path to deepen our understanding of the dreaming process. It can also be useful for you and me.

Dreaming is a methodology or channel for increasing our awareness, we are able to accomplish multidimensional travel, seek consultation and wisdom and set us on a foundation and course for an expansive and elevated existence. Dreaming, then, is not a passive act, a secondary activity to sleep, a process of random images, but is or can be a life altering experience that can not only enrich our lives but can amplify our spirituality and instruct us on how to live ethically, peacefully, and more fully. Castaneda's work and recording of his experiences with Matus has added so much not only to the study of anthropology, but more importantly to the study of how spirit work and interacts with us in human form.

"FROM THE CONSERVATIVE ASSUMPTION OF THREE REM PERIODS PER NIGHT AND TWO DREAM STORIES WITHIN EACH PERIOD, THERE IS A RESULTANT 150,000 DREAMS PER PERSON OVER A LIFE SPAN OF 70 YEARS."

Wilse B. Webb

Chapter 9

DREAMS AS A MEANS OF COMMUNICATING WITH DEPARTED LOVED ONES

Communicating with loved ones, through dreams, has long been realized and accepted throughout time and traditions. In my own dreams, my mother comes when she has something she wants me to do or when she has a message for me. Shortly after my mother's death, she came to me in a dream, angry because she did not have a tombstone on her grave. She said and I quote, "This does not make any sense. I have four educated daughters and I don't have a tombstone." She was very upset that a woman of her stature "God's Woman" was treated in such a manner. She considered it very disrespectful and dishonoring. I was reminded of a biblical passage "Honor thy father and mother that thou days may be long on the earth."

On another occasion, after I had appeased her, she appeared in my dream and told me that she would help me do my spiritual work. In the African Tradition it is believed that the community consists also of the ancestor that offers guidance and protection to their living family members.

I had another encounter with a friend that died leaving two young children. My friend, Patty, in life was a talented interior decorator and designer. In the dream I had about her, she was still designing and decorating houses, but on a larger scale. It appears that your talents follow you through death and continue on a greater level. At the end of the visit with Patty, she asked me to check on her children.

Similarly, I had another dream with a friend, Denise. What is so interesting about Denise's death is that we met for dinner a few weeks before her transition, where we had a conversation about dreams and communicating with departed loved ones. She said that her ex-husband came to her after his death. He died relatively early (in his 40s) and in the dream Denise said that when her husband came she said to him, " I thought you were dead." "He said I don't want to talk about that." After she died, she came to me in a dream and also asked me to check on her son, who had not finished high school at the time of her death. It appears that mothers are very concerned about their children particularly if they are young.

When my grandmother died, she came to me in a dream within one weak after her passing. She was dressed in white; her hair and skin were shining. She looked young and new. My grandmother said nothing to me. Sometimes I think this was a vision as opposed to a dream because there was no talking or story, or issue. She appeared in her glorified body and just seeing her in all of her glory gave me such a feeling of peace. This vision I shared with my loved ones about her let them know that she was fine and living her life after death.

Loved ones also come in dreams to comfort their families and friends. I spoke to a friend who lives in New York about two months after her husband passed away. I asked her if he had come to her yet and she said that he had come twice. Once he came to engage in sexual activity with her. She thought he came to have sex with her as a means to comfort her and so that he may remain close to her. She said that he came on another occasion to calm her down when she was upset with another family member. He assured her that everything would work out.

I consulted with a female minister, Lorine, about her

encounter with dreams. She said that her mother and sister come to her when there are family issues, and when she is ill her grandmother comes to her assistance. She believes dreaming is a primary way that the departed can communicate with the ones they love which also suggests and implies that relationships continue after death and love has the capacity to survive death.

I spoke with one of my male friends to inquire if he communicates with departed love ones. He told me of a situation where his mother came with her opinion about some property he and his sister where considering purchasing in South Florida. He said that his mother said, "I don't know why you want to spend so much money on an apartment anyway." This dream helped them not to pursue this business deal. Ancestor's and loved ones come with warnings and messages.

If you would like to communicate with a loved one, you can make an alter for them with a picture, flowers, candles or with their personal effects, or you can spend some time thinking about them. If you would like to continue with this level of dialog or communication, remove your fear and ask them to come to you. You may also write them a letter and express how you feel and ask any questions that you have.

Sometimes loved ones will come to you if they had a painful death or if there was foul play involved in their death. They want to be justified and appeased and sometimes they come to a loved one for them to listen to them or to request assistance in receiving justice and understanding. You may help them to receive comfort and to move on by praying for them and loving them unconditionally. Even if you feel their death was partly their fault.

Again, relationships can continue pasts the veil of what we call death and provide continuity and family and friendship ties. Additionally, loved ones, on the other side, are able to better grasp the bigger picture and can assist their loved ones with making difficult decisions, and a host of difficult issues and problems.

THE WORD

The word became alive and appeared before me
Bare
Naked and
Real.
I molded them, shaped them and handled them well.
Its manifestation was as a mirror- a reflection of my
own thoughts, my own creation.

Find your words and you find your way. Find your way
and you find your world. Select both wisely for they
become your truth.

In the beginning was the word and the word became
flesh and dwelt amongst us. Our future is determined
by our words. They can be friend or foe, your
guardian angel or your demon of destruction.

Words are your clay to be shaped as you please and
thoughts and imaginations are the patterns that cut a
path to your destiny. It is how word, thought and
imagination meet that determines the shape of your life.

Phyllis Baker

Chapter 10

CONNECTING THE DREAM WITH THE WORD
"AN AFRICAN CONTEXT"

"Writing is one matter and knowledge is another. Writing is the photograph of knowledge but is not knowledge itself. Knowledge is a light that is in man. It is the heritage of all that our ancestors have known, and it is in the gem they transmit to us; just a baobab-tree is potentially in its seed." This is from traditionalist, Tierno Bokar. (Bâ, 1989 p.168)

Africa is a continent that is often known for its oral practices for translating information. Africa is now accepted as the birthplace of humanity. As a result, it has embodied and maintained many ancient spiritual treasures that we are just beginning to explore and unravel. I was struck with the work of A. Hampaté Bâ titled, "The Living Tradition." In it, he so excellently describes the power of the spoken Word and I thought it would be a great starting point for me to draw from the African tradition and its usefulness for opening up channels to the unconsciousness and as a result to our dreams.

"When we speak of African tradition or history we mean oral tradition; and no attempt at penetrating the history and spirit of the African peoples is valid unless it relies on that heritage of knowledge of every kind. Patiently transmitted from mouth to ear, from master to disciple, down through the ages, this heritage is not yet lost, but lies there in the memory of the last generation of great depositories, of whom it can be said: They are the living memory of Africa." (Bâ, 1989 p.167)

According to Bâ there is a sacred bond that connects human kind to words. There is a sacred character associated with its divine origin. Speaking words are like casting a magical spell and must not be taken lightly.

With this thought in mind, we must remember to always speak positive words, which are activated by a positive mind and outlook. We should talk about promise, joy, life, health, prosperity and peace. Don't say anything negative.

Oral tradition is the school of life, all aspects of which are covered and affected by it. It may, also, seem chaos to those who do not penetrate its secret; it may baffle the Cartesian mind accustomed to dividing everything up into clear-cut categories. In oral tradition, in fact, spiritual and material are not dissociated". (Ba, p168)

In the Biblical creation story the world began with the word, with G-D speaking the word. Human speech sets forces into action and is viewed in African as a gift from God. Speech in the African Tradition is the greatest agent in African Magic. Magic is defined as the "Management of Forces." In the African Tradition speech derives the essence of its power from the sacred and it is believed that rupture occurs in the harmony of humankind and their society, when one's words are impure. In most traditional oral societies, lying is considered moral leprosy and the occult part of the person dies from lying. Generally speaking, traditional Africans "have a horror of the lie." (Bâ)

In chapter twelve, you will be given words to speak and later you will be asked to come up with your own words that are given to you from the cosmic mind. These words may be yours or they may be words from inspired beings that would allow you to properly request information from the unconscious that you need to know for healing, growth, cleansing and transformation.

In chapter 12, you will also be asked to encounter and document a 12 day and night dream journey. Ritualize and enrich this activity with utilizing any or all of the four elements, i.e., earth, wind, fire and water. Be sure to light a candle before speaking your words and at the end of the process blow out the candle. This ritual will cement the process into consciousness and cause a shift in attitude and behavior. You may choose to include additional elements of feelings and activity to the process as extra tools to help penetrate the dreaming process whereby allowing for better dream reception.

A point of caution, before you begin this African based practice you cannot judge everything according to your own criteria. To discover a new world, you must open your heart to the secrets of the ages that are found and disbursed in diverse peoples and diverse cultures.

One further note before we leave this section. African Traditionalist would suggest we repeat our affirmation or incantations in a rhythmic manner. It is believed that the "to and fro" method adds movement and dimension to the ritual, thereby, strengthening, enhancing and giving more power to the word.

"In the beginning was the word."(Genesis) Speak the word!

**"UNLESS THE PRINCIPLES ARE PRAC-
TICED, THEY REMAIN SPECULATIVE THEO-
RIES."**

Dr. Mary Tumpkins

Chapter 11

PUT YOUR DREAM TO THE TEST!

In order to able to bring our dream life into focus and to demonstrate our dreams there has to be first and foremost a CENTERING PROCESS. Your center can be based on your religious belief, your philosophical beliefs, your scientific beliefs or your statement of purpose. This is your grounding, for your tree if it is to produce fruit, must have roots. If you are to receive information in your dreams, the content is much more coherent if filtered through a context and channel that is connected to the source. Everyone does not perceive this source in the same way. We have our cul tural, religious, and individual frames of references that are different from person to person. Everyone is not comfortable with the God question and God answers and is more comfortable with the concept of "Energy." Colleen Deatsman, author of *Energy for Life: Connect with the Source* offers the following:

Energy...a brief history

Although there are no written records, it seems clear that the earliest humans understood the fundamentals of energy. Archaeological evidence and early cave paintings indicate that water, wind, earth and fire all figured prominently in the daily lives of the people of prehistory. The one other fascinating thing about these records is the presence of the unseen. It would appear that, from the earliest humans, our species had an instinctual understanding that there are unseen forces at work. As early people organized into groups, then civilization, they evolved their explanations of the unseen to fit the context of their own level of development.

Ancient texts, teachings, and practices reveal that every culture's tradition, religion, and spiritual path has (or had) at its root an understanding that energy is the force of life. Many of our ancient roots regarding energy are found in the practice of shamanism.

Shamanism has always been a bridge between what is seen and what is unseen, and is a path whose deepest core belief is animism. Animism is the understanding that all things are living, connected and are interconnected by an energy force called the web of life. All of manifest existence has a soul…plants, animals, birds, this book, the chair you are sitting on, and you and me. Shamanism represents the most widespread and ancient methodological system of energy healing known to humanity, and is thought to have predated and been incorporated into all spiritualities and religions. This means that all of our great spiritual and religious traditions have at their base an understanding that everything is energy.

About four thousand years ago, ancient sages began to refine and document a practice of introspection that had sprung from rituals of this prehistoric Shamanism. The transcendent nature of energy was discovered when the ancient sages began to analyze the nature of consciousness. Insights gained from these practices explained the forces of nature and the nature of the self in terms of energy. These ancient sages, the Vedics of the Indus Valley in India, clearly drew on their traditional Shamanism beliefs and combined these animist beliefs with their research into their own bodies, minds souls, and spirits. The result was one of the most luminous texts ever produced- the Rig Veda. This text explained the seen and unseen as proceeding from a common genesis. That genesis was pure, high powered, intelligent universal life force energy. The Vedics claimed that this energy, pregnant with potential and driven to create, is the fundamental engine of creation. The product of this creation is the universe and everything in it, having been created by combining dense, elemental energies into more complex structures. The upshot of all this is that the divine source energy, in its drive to create, formed an energetic structure as a background to the universe upon which all of manifest existence dances. According to the Rig Veda, this divine, blind impulse densifies and evolves; moving across the web of life, until it can finds its way back, aware of itself this time, to formless divine. Like the prodigal son in the Christian parable, the return of this self-awareness energy, full of its acquired understanding is cause for great celebration in the Vedic celestial sphere.

This concept of descent and rebirth is probably the most common mythical element in the history of mankind. It seems to be hard-wired right into our DNA. Every major mythology in the world includes it. The Hebrew Qabala reflects this energetic descent and return. Christian convention addresses the descent into purgatory accompanied by the ultimate rebirth into heaven. Taoist and Buddhist teachings reflect an awakening from a dull sleep into vibrate awareness. Sufism speaks rapturously of a reintegrating reunion with the divine after a descent into this world. Every one of these presents a methodology for how to bring this transformation about. Each has its own set of ideas about how to improve and enhance those personal attributes it considers valuable, and how to minimize those characteristics that diminish us. In other words, nearly every belief system in the history of the world represents a method for how to become lighter and brighter and power-filled in a world that seems full of things that drain and darken. They each give us recommendations about how to best utilize the energy we have and how with practice, to dip into the infinite well of divine energy.

"Energy for Life: Connect with the Source"
By Colleen Deatsman

I thought I would include this segment by Colleen

Deatsman, <u>Energy for Life,</u> for context. I think this essay provides an explanation that religious and non-religious persons can possibly embrace. It serves as a foundational principle that could lend itself to the centering process. The centering process, again, is based on what you believe and hold as your truth and the principles by which you live. Some people are very comfortable with a belief in God and others are not. This principle is the starting point, the center, the source and subsequent dreams can be based on or filtered through that premise. Utilizing this approach will require you to become a metaphysical, even a spiritual scientist. Your mind is your laboratory in which you conduct various experiments. You must be just as intent in discovering yourself as the scientist is trying to find a cure for cancer. You must be willing to look through the microscope of your mind to find the tiniest elements because those elements are the building blocks by which you develop your dream consciousness. Pay attention to themes, feelings, unctions, directives, people, messengers, signs, symbols, colors, animals, sounds, lights, pictures, and landscapes.

In calculating your dreams, you can began with the big picture and reduce the picture down to a common denominator and common theme. Yes, you can begin with a feeling or a theme and began to ask yourself some questions. Why do I feel so blue? What am I being propelled or asked to do? Why is this person showing up in my dreams? If it works better, you may start with the small elements; it may be a word or an object or a color that is revealed or a person who shows up in the dream. The total vista of the dream has to be developed, through the process of amplification, expansion and dialog with the dream. It is recommended again that you don't move immediately when you awake, for you must transfer the content of the dream from the unconscious to the conscious state of mind.

After the transfer is made, you may begin to write the dream down or speak the dream into a tape recorder. The intuition operates like a flash if you move too fast or move too slow, you miss out on what the super mind is saying to you. You should be fully present in the dream...fully conscious. You must use parts of yourself that you have not discovered yet. This is my definition of growth for being able to capture and use more of your dreams is learning how to use more and more of your mind; remember it is said that we use so little of it, only ten or fifteen percent. There is room and space for more use. Dive into the dream; watch and observe the dream, be just like the creator, for there is a part of you that never sleeps that never slumbers that is the G_d force that resides within each and every one of us. For deep down inside of us something is trying, truly trying to tell us something.

As you prepare yourself to be enriched and elevated in your dream life, I recommend the following steps and actions:

1. Get Ready to Dream by facilitating your space.
Take a bath to minimize the physical body's obstructions and discomfort to the sleeping and dreaming process. This makes it easier on yourself; it makes you feel better. Clean your room and make it soothing and relaxing. Fix it up and make it your temple... your sleeping and dreaming sanctuary.

2. Feel the Dream.

You must feel your dream like you feel the sensation of hot and cold. This requires that you are present, you are there; you are conscious. Embrace the dream experience like you would embrace a beloved teacher or a true friend. Your dreams are your teacher; they are your friend, they are you. "Behold now I stand at the door and knock." Please let the dream come in. This is a divine opportunity to reveal a part of you that has been hidden. We have mistreated our dreams, for we have refused them, abused them, distrusted them and underutilized them. Embrace your dreams. Let them in by welcoming them as you would a dear part of the family. They will add to your being and serve as an important resource and guide. Why do we pretend to be so tough, when the truth of the matter is that we all need help, direction, and strength?

3. Receive the Dream

Believe that it is the deep communication of your mind and soul. Give the dream a place in your life. Write it down, talk to it; it will holler back. At that point, dialogue can be established and maintained. Maintaining your dream relationship is like any other relationship. It will wither and die if we don't take care of them, embrace them, and have fellowship and communion with them.

4. Obey the dream by participating and by action.

For our dreams should propel us to act, to move. This is how the dream becomes flesh and lives within us and for us.

5. Enjoy the Dream!

Like you enjoy your favorite movie or television program, also enjoy your dreams. When we have developed such an interest or appreciation for a program or movie, we scheduled it into our day. We watch attentively, we laugh, cry, reflect, learn and are many times entertained. Why not engage in a similar activity when you dream where you are the producer, director and in most cases the actor staring in you own movie or documentary, where you can record or document aspects of your life. Many movies and books, great works of art, movements, and ideas come from one's dream. We must learn to appreciate the script that is being manufactured by us.

You don't have to be a dream expert to begin. Start where you are, start right here, right now if you like, start with this book. For it is a reminder of a gift that we have left behind, we forgot about, or did not realize its true value. For our dreams are like diamonds, many times like diamonds in the rough, but by discovery, cultivation and polish they will shine bright for us.

We learn thru trial and error to develop our dream hypothesis. This requires becoming a student of your dreams and good students study, read and investigate. Your dreams will allow you to investigate yourself.

"Dream the Dream"

Phyllis Baker

Chapter 12

YOUR DREAM JOURNEY

Instructions: Tonight Began Your Dream Journey. Limit or eliminate your alcoholic intake during this period. Eat lightly before retiring. Minimize sugar and highly seasoned foods. Include natural juices, fruits and vegetables in your diet. Engage in some form of exercise on a regular bases. Walk, run, swim, dance, jump rope or participate in an activity that you enjoy. If you have hatred or negativity in your life surrender, forgive, and release it. Drink plenty of water to flush toxins out of your system. Optional: You may light a candle and after you repeat these affirmations write them down and place them underneath your pillow. If you have a pressing need or problem you may meditate and fast (abstain from food and negativity during this phase.)

NIGHT NUMBER ONE
NIGHT OF ANTICIPATION

Please repeat this affirmation.
Tonight I will sleep with my eyes open.
Tonight I will sleep with my ears open.
Tonight I will sleep with my heart open.
Show me, speak to me, and teach me.

The next day when you wake up write anything you remember here:

_____
_____
_____
_____
_____
_____
_____
_____
_____
_____
_____
_____
_____

NIGHT NUMBER TWO
"NIGHT OF WONDER"

Affirmation: *Please repeat the following:*
I am waiting at the dream port ready to take my ride.
Drive and direct me to that place I need to go, see, and
experience.
Record your dream and your response to your dream
here.

_____
_____
_____
_____
_____
_____
_____
_____
_____
_____
_____
_____
_____
_____
_____
_____
_____

NIGHT NUMBER THREE
"NIGHT OF REFLECTION"

Affirmation: *Please repeat the following:*

I affirm my right to know.
I affirm my right to see.
I affirm my right to be all I can be.
Send me a message tonight.
Record your dream and your response to the dream here.

_____

_____

_____

_____

_____

_____

_____

_____

_____

_____

_____

_____

_____

_____

_____

_____

_____

_____

_____

_____

_____

_____

NIGHT NUMBER FOUR
"NIGHT OF ILLUMINATION"

Affirmation: *Please repeat the following:*
I have talents that reside in the realm of the
unknown. Reveal to me what they are and allow me to see
myself embracing and demonstrating the talents that I
have.
Show me.
Show me.
Show me.
Record your dream and your response here.

_____

_____

_____

_____

_____

_____

_____

_____

_____

_____

_____

_____

_____

_____

_____

_____

_____

_____

_____

_____

NIGHT NUMBER FIVE
"THE NIGHT OF PSYCHOLOGICAL RESOLU-TION"

Affirmation: *Repeat these words:*
I need to know those things, people, and events that
I must release from my psyche so I can move on to
my greatest and highest good. Help me accept.
Help me be strong.
Help me move on.
Record your dream and response here.

_____
_____
_____
_____
_____
_____
_____
_____
_____
_____
_____
_____
_____
_____
_____
_____
_____
_____
_____

NIGHT NUMBER SIX
"NIGHT OF FUN"

Affirmation: *Please repeat the following:*
I would like to have fun.
Provide me dream master with a good fun dream
tonight.
Record your dream and response here.

_____

_____

_____

_____

_____

_____

_____

_____

_____

_____

_____

_____

_____

_____

_____

_____

_____

_____

_____

_____

_____

_____

_____

_____

NIGHT NUMBER SEVEN
"NIGHT OF REST."

Affirmation: *Please repeat these words:*
I need rest for my soul. Allow me to rest like never
before. I am safe; I am secure, and satisfied.
Sleep.
Rest.
Relax.
Record your dream and response
here.

_____

_____

_____

_____

_____

_____

_____

_____

_____

_____

_____

_____

_____

_____

_____

_____

_____

_____

_____

_____

Florida International University
11000 SW 8th Street
Miami, FL 33174
305-348-2691

Barnes & Noble at FIU

STORE:07550   REG:019   TRAN#:075
CASHIER:KERWING R

BAKER/DREAMER'S JO
NEW
9781584324713   1
                    (1 @ 20.00)   20.00

Subtotal   20.00
T1 Sales Tax (07.000%)   1.40
TOTAL   21.40
ATM DEBIT   21.40
Card#: XXXXXXXXXXXXX1870

All text book sales are final

V240.50   01/20/2012 01:09PM

with original receipt.
- With proof of a schedule change and original receipt, a full refund will be given in your original form of payment during the first 30 days of classes.
- No refunds on unwrapped loose leaf books or activated eBooks.
- Textbooks must be in original condition.
- No refunds or exchanges without original receipt.

GENERAL READING BOOKS, SOFTWARE, AUDIO, VIDEO & SMALL ELECTRONICS
- A full refund will be given in your original form of payment if merchandise is returned within 14 days of purchase with original receipt.
- Opened software, audio books, DVDs, CDs, music, and small electronics may not be returned. They can be exchanged for the same item if defective.
- Merchandise must be in original condition.
- No refunds or exchanges without original receipt.

ALL OTHER MERCHANDISE
- A full refund will be given in your original form of payment with original receipt.
- Without a receipt, a store credit will be issued at the current selling price.
- Cash back on merchandise credits or gift cards will not exceed $1.
- No refunds on gift cards, prepaid cards, phone cards, newspapers, or magazines.
- Merchandise must be in original condition.

Fair Pricing Policy
Barnes & Noble College Booksellers comply with local weights & measures requirements. If the price on your receipt is above the advertised or posted price, please alert a bookseller and we will gladly refund the difference.

REFUND POLICY

TEXTBOOKS:
- A full refund will be given in your original form of payment if textbooks are returned during the first week of classes with original receipt.
- With proof of a schedule change and original receipt, a full refund will be given in your original form of payment during the first 30 days of classes.
- No refunds on unwrapped loose leaf books
- Textbooks must be in original condition.

NIGHT NUMBER EIGHT
"NIGHT OF HEALING"

Affirmation: *Please repeat the following:*
I accept my healing tonight.
Record your dream and your response here.

_____

_____

_____

_____

_____

_____

_____

_____

_____

_____

_____

_____

_____

_____

_____

_____

_____

_____

_____

_____

_____

_____

NIGHT NUMBER NINE
"THE NIGHT OF WISH FULFILL MENT"

Affirmation: I cast my desire
for_____ (make your request
here) before you dear spirit and ask for its manifes-
tation.
I believe!
I believe!
I receive!
Record your dream and response here.

_____

_____

_____

_____

_____

_____

_____

_____

_____

_____

_____

_____

_____

_____

_____

_____

_____

_____

_____

_____

_____

NIGHT NUMBER TEN
"THE NIGHT OF INTELLECT"

Affirmation: Activate and stimulate my intellect whereby I can clearly perceive and understand. Record your dream and response here.

_____

_____

_____

_____

_____

_____

_____

_____

_____

_____

_____

_____

_____

_____

_____

_____

_____

_____

_____

_____

_____

_____

_____

_____

_____

_____

_____

NIGHT NUMBER ELEVEN
"NIGHT OF PROBLEM SOLVING"

Affirmation: *Please repeat the following:*
There are problems that must be solved.
Elevate me to the challenge.
Reveal the answers.
Order my steps.
Lead the way.
Record your dream and your response here.

_____
_____
_____
_____
_____
_____
_____
_____
_____
_____
_____
_____
_____
_____
_____
_____
_____
_____
_____
_____
_____
_____

NIGHT NUMBER TWELVE
"NIGHT OF SPIRITUAL GROWTH"

Affirmation: *Please repeat the following:*
Oh Divine light shine on me and allow me to behold my
Spiritual path.
Show me my path,
Help me to embrace my path and
Follow my path.
Record your dream and response here.

_____

_____

_____

_____

_____

_____

_____

_____

_____

_____

_____

_____

_____

_____

_____

_____

_____

_____

_____

_____

_____

_____

"AND BEING WARNED IN A DREAM THAT THEY
SHOULD NOT RETURN TO HEROLD, THEY
RETURNED TO THEIR OWN COUNTRY BY A DIF-
FERENT ROUTE"

Matthew 2:12

Chapter 13

MY DREAMS

Night One August 13, 2007

In my dream tonight I was attending a huge and what appeared to be Pentecostal Healing Service. It is very interesting that the dream came to me in this way because I was raised with this tradition. Many of my relatives are a part of the religion and I still draw on aspects of it. In the service demons are being casted out. I saw a being that appeared to be half human and half beast, and holy people are standing around this creature casting out an evil spirit.

During the healing session I watched most of the service from the other room and on a television monitor. In an adjacent room I am sitting with two women. One I cannot remember and the other was a friend I have known for several years. We were having a conversation, but I am not sure what about. I offered to get tea or coffee for the ladies. I went inside the church looking for coffee for the other lady and tea for Ms. Lo. I see a man coming out of the church with a large coffee pot. In the Pot he only had hot water. So I get the Hot Water for Ms. Lo.

The message that I received from this dream is that the person that was being healed was a common friend who had on occasions been mean spirited to both of us. Something needs to heal as it relates to that relationship.

I believe this message came to me last night because this is a first order of business in that I will see this person this weekend for an activity, after not seeing him for over a year and I must prepare myself for this meeting. As a result of my dream, I am seeking peace and reconciliation.

"This peace I leave with you surpasses all human understanding"
Deliverance is at hand.
Deliverance is at hand.

Night Two August 16, 2007
Tonight or rather early in the morning of August 16, 2007 my dream was about my family. However, the only person that I really remember in the dream was my son, Robert. I know other family members were there but their

faces were not clear to me. We were on vacation in a cottage near the Everglades. My son, in the dream, was not his current age but much younger, between 8 and12 years of age. He was his funny and playful self, innocent and curious.

His love for animals was clear in the dream for he was actively looking for all the animals he could find. He was fascinated with monkeys there and showed an interest in all the animals. He had that look of wonder on his face. He also loved spending time and playing with the other children living at the cottage and was thrilled by the food there, especially the desserts.

My son and I have been having some disagreements lately. I felt disappointed that he is considering not going to school this semester. I am concerned that the student loan that I co-signed for will become due and payable. I discussed this with my son about two weeks ago, and it ended up being a very heart-felt discussion. In this dream, I saw my son in a better light. I was reminded of why I love him. I remember the early days of our mother/child relationship…but he is no longer a child. I must accept that also.

I believe this dream is telling me to trust my son that he is working out his life right now in the best way he can. I gleaned that I must embrace my son's innocence, natural curiosity and goodness.

Night Three August 26, 2007
Tonight I dreamed about my father, Mr. Abner Stripling, (1911-1982) In the dream, I visited my father in his barber shop, but the shop was in another place, and another dimension. My dad was cutting a young man's hair

and, at the same time, talking with my uncle Rev. Arletha Sermons, my mother's brother. He was visiting. My uncle and I did not talk in the dream; I only spoke with my father. When I walked in I gave my dad a hug and was glad to see him for I had not seen him in quite awhile. The conversation was very short but my father said, "Don't forget about me." As a result I would like to tell you about my father.

My father was a refined and dignified man. He was an entrepreneur, a barber, a community activist, and a very good father. He was committed to his family, church, and community. My father set the tone for my academic life, for he encouraged education, self-respect, moral development and activism. My father was a member of the NAACP an organization that worked to end segregation, challenge discrimination and the mistreatment of African-Americans. I remember, as a youth, my father going to Washington, DC to participate with the Reverend Martin Luther King Jr. on the historical March on Washington. What excitement to know that my father was one of those in a movement that assisted in the liberation of my people!

My father owned a business that consisted of a barbershop and beauty salon. It was more than a business; it was a community and education center where people felt free to come in and talk things over. They participated in stimulating and engaging discussions and developed networks for personal and professional growth. My father owned other property in the neighborhood, and as a result was responsible for me and some of my other siblings inheriting and owning homes and property. This was primarily my father's doing because my mother did not work. My father was largely a self-educated man. I say largely self-educated because no man is an island; no man stands alone. He insisted that all five of his children go to college and, as a result, four graduated college and three have advanced degrees. We attribute this largely to our father.

He wrote excellent poetic and profound speeches that he could deliver with passion and from memory at various church events. He was a forthright, charming, in my estimation a brilliant man. Thanks daddy for helping me become the woman that I am.

Night Four August 28, 2007
The focus of tonight's dream was symbols and the importance of understanding your own symbolic language. In your dreams you can learn that people, animals, words, colors, and other aspects of life have a meaning or have symbols that have representation of meaning. In my dream tonight I had an encounter with two men, both of which I know. Carlos appeared in the dream, which was unusual because I only see him a few times of year. Carlos, in the dream, represented or had characteristics of a deeply spiritual being, his energy and vibration in the dream was very positive and angelic.

The other man in the dream I will call him Mr. Dee. He was very negative in the dream, and he had devious animals with him. The animals appeared as monkeys, which along with Mr. Dee for me represented the shadow (dark side) and the trickster in this dream. There were several words that appear as visuals in the dream. All the words in the dream were power words that resonated with me. Many of the words I forgot, but the word I remember was "CONSCIOUNESS." The word felt good and this word I plan to use more in my writing and my speech.

I learned in this dream to pay attention to the vibrations of the symbols given in dreams. These symbols can lead you to the good and teach you how to minimize the negative forces in our environment. From this dream, I surmised that there must be hundreds and thousands of other symbols from which we can gain a better understanding.

Night Number 5 August 29, 2007

This dream came during the morning after I had my morning bike ride. I also had gone grocery shopping that morning and decided that I would go back to bed and get another hour of sleep. In the dream I was with my family and another family was with us. We had a day of activity and the other family decided to follow us. I was driving and following the other family. As we were getting off of the highway, I began to feel light headed and I almost ran into their car. I got out of the car so that my son could drive for me. The gentleman of the other family accompanied me to my town house to have a look at my television, which was broken. My family and his family were in another location. I began to feel lightheaded again and reminded him of the earlier incident. He recommended, at that point, that I take an aspirin.

When I woke up, I did have a headache and felt light headed. I immediately got a glass of water and took an aspirin. I went back to sleep for about an hour. When I woke up this time there was no sign of a headache or the discomfort I had. This was a health related dream, where I was instructed what to do to feel better and to maintain my health. I have had other experiences in my dreams where I was given instructions to health related matters. Sometimes I am advised to go to the doctor. A few times I was guided to use some aloe. (Plant) On other occasions I have been lead to use goldenseal. (Herb)

Dreams can be a wonderful vehicle to help us maintain health, vitality and energy. Your dreams can tell you things about your health and your cures and remedies. Many times we are not aware of these remedies or they are out of mind. Dreams are a beautiful reminder. The question is: Are we willing to invest the time, focus, and energy to listen and attune to our dream? Don't forget to take guidance from your dreams for they have the potential to help in so many areas.

Conclusion

DREAMS AS THERAPY

Dreams have the amazing ability to teach, warn, inspire, guide and direct, minimize our neurosis and cause a catharsis in the human personality and soul. Dreams can help us more if we can access them, pay attention to them, and understand how to apply what we have learned from the dream.

We can access the dream by facilitating a dream life. First of all, we must understand that dreams can have validity and there have been prophetic and precognitive dreams associated with all culture, religions, ages, professions and nationalities. You have now a basic understanding of how dreams have been used in various practices and other spiritual domains, in the psychological arena, in the creative arena, and in everyday usage for everyday people. The beauty of dreams is that they have universal application. There is no discrimination, and understanding this fact, one can use the power of faith, imagination and rational thought as the dream incubator for enhancing this ability. Through the process of self instruction, will, focused attention and desire, you can begin to provoke the dream. We have very strong minds; we must give the brain and the spirit a charge and an assignment. If you have difficulty, draw on the tools that you have learned in this book. Be sure to use your dream affirmations, because by speaking them and writing those down you make a greater impression on the subconscious mind.

When we are dreaming we must remember to remember what we saw, heard, and experienced in the dream. We must pay attention to our attention. We must use the power of recollection and memory to assist us. In the dream process you are not only the participant; you are the observer and the recorder of the dream. As you become a more skilled dreamer, you can confront your fears, desires, fault, and your dark side. While dreaming, you can begin to ask yourself questions. Such as why are you afraid of this? Why am I not acting in this situation? Why am I in pain? What must I do to be healed? You can also ask for help to assist you in making difficult decisions and to make hard choices and changes. You must become conversant with the dream and with yourself.

Don't be afraid to talk to yourself when you are dreaming… listen, speak, ask for assistance, the higher self will help and guide you. This important dialog is part and parcel of dream therapy and will allow you to come to terms with many important aspects of your self. You will confront the dream and the dream will confront you. Being afraid or hiding from the dream will not help us overcome the various aspects about ourselves and of life that keep us in pain and minimize our ability to live fully, joyously, and in peace. We must gather ourselves, look our fears and demons in the face and say "What?" We must approach our higher self in the dream and say, "Yes!" These conversations are possible and necessary in our dream life if we want to have integrated, whole, and self actualized existences. This intervention can lead us to emotional, psychological, physical and spiritual health.

Journaling will allow you to remember your dreams and keep better records of your growth and development. By writing your dreams down you can look at yourself from a larger perspective. You can gain better knowledge of your dream language and symbols. Sometimes your dreams come in riddles that have to be solved. By writing your dreams down, you can contemplate the riddle or the meanings, themes, and emotions you experience in the dream. What issues and people keep coming up in the dream? You need to know why. Journaling can also help you keep track of your process. What issues have you overcome? What hurdles have you crossed? What issues are now mute issues or non-issues? Journaling can assist you in drawing parallels and recount your precognitive dreams and abilities. With these tools you are better prepared to see yourself and your life from a more holistic perspective. You are then allowed to put the pieces of your psyche together, to make sense to yourself, to know yourself in deeper and more meaningful ways. As a result, you can cure many of your ills and address many of your own concerns. In a real sense, you can facilitate your own transformations and your own therapeutic processes by working with your dreams.

Our dreams are gifts. They are sacred resources given to us by the creator so we can live a purposeful, informed and happy life. Dreams will allow us the ability to know what's going on with ourselves and those in our world. Being armed with information, awareness, power, we are in a much better position to move forward.

References

Bâ, H.   The Living Tradition (article) Methodology and African Prehistory, Joseph Zerbo, Editor, University of California Press, 1989

Baker, P. African-American Spirituality, Thought & Culture. IUniverse, 2007

Carskadon, M. A. Encyclopedia of Sleep and dreaming. New York: Macmillan, 1993

Castaneda, C. The Art of Dreaming. New York: Harper Collins, 1993

Deatsman, C. Energy for Life: Connect with the Source. Lewellyn World Wide. St. Paul, MN, 2006

Dement, W.C. & Vanghan, C. The Promise of Sleep. New York: Delacorte, 1999

Douglas, R. Decoding Your Dreams. New York: Sterling Publishing Co Inc, 2005

Fontana, D. The Secret Language of Dreams. San Francisco: Chronicle Books, 1991.

Freud, S. The Interpretation of Dreams. New York: Harper Collins Publisher, 1998

Hall, C.S. The Sigmund Freud Primer. New York: Harper Collins Publisher, 1999

Harner, M. The Way of the Shaman. New York: Harper

Collins, 1990

Jung, C. <u>Man and His Symbols.</u> New York: Dell
Publishing, 1964

Kassin, S. <u>Psychology.</u> New Jersey: Prentice Hall 3rd ed.
2001

Puryear, H.B. <u>The Edgar Cayce Primer: Discovering the
Path to Self-Transformation.</u> New York: Bantam Books,
1982

Van De Castle, R. <u>Our Dreaming Mind</u>. New York:
Ballantine Books, 1994

Vollmar, K. <u>The Little Giant Encyclopedia of Dream
Symbols. New York:</u> Sterling Publishing Co., 1997.